Civil Rights Coloring Book

Includes Activities!

By Carole Marsh

Written by Carole Marsh; Illustrations by Yvonne Ford

Imagine that you want to eat in a restaurant, but you can't go inside because of your skin color. Imagine that you want to ride a city bus, but you have to sit in the back because of your skin color. Imagine that you just want a cool drink of water on sweltering afternoon, but you can't drink from the water fountain because of your skin color.

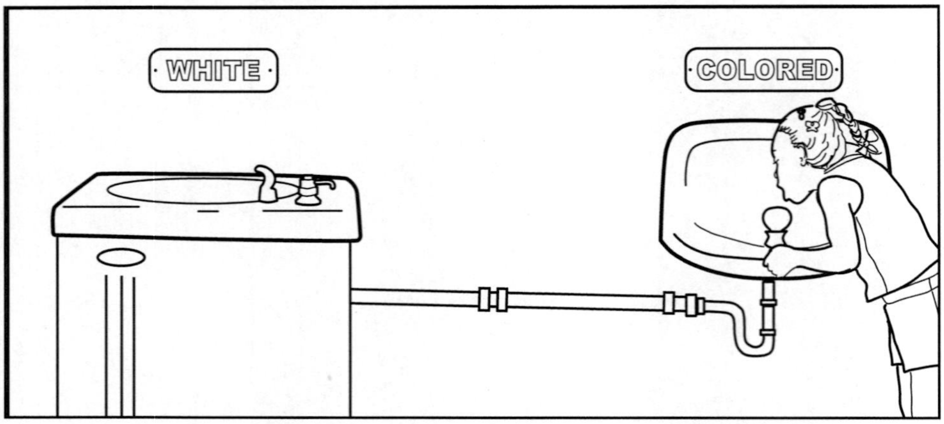

Those examples are all make-believe, right? No, they're not! They were facts of life for many African Americans in the United States during the early and mid-1900s.

Laws separated African Americans from white Americans in most public places. That included restaurants, hotels, schools, bathrooms, and even doctors' offices! The pictures on this page show the type of signs that people saw when they went to public places.

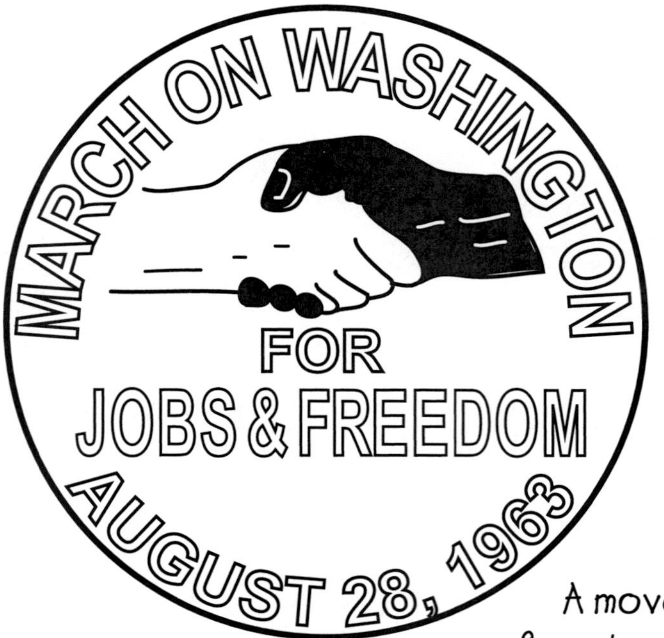

African Americans wanted to change the laws. Many white Americans did, too! African Americans deserved the same rights as all other Americans. They wanted freedom to do what they wanted and go where they wanted. They wanted to have the same opportunities for jobs and education as everyone else!

A movement for freedom rose up in America. During the Civil Rights Movement, many people spoke out for equal rights and equal opportunities. African Americans got attention by breaking the laws designed to keep them separated. It took years and years of struggle to make a difference—but it happened! Finally, the laws were changed!

WHAT ARE CIVIL RIGHTS?

Civil rights are the rights that every person should have, regardless of his or her gender, race, or religion.

Jackie Robinson was the first African American to play major-league baseball. Many people were mean to him, but he was strong! He opened the door for Black athletes in all sports. Play ball!

Tuskegee Airmen

The Tuskegee Airmen were the first Black military airmen to serve in the U.S. armed forces. They helped create opportunities for African Americans in the U.S. military.

Third-grader Linda Brown wanted to go to an all-white school close to her house. The principal said no. Her dad went to court and won! After that, Black and white children could go to school together.

Nine Black students wanted to go to a white high school in Arkansas. The governor said no, but President Eisenhower said yes! He sent soldiers to escort the "Little Rock Nine" into the school.

Rosa Parks rode the bus to and from work in Montgomery, Alabama. She sat in the Black section. One day, a white man wanted Rosa to give him her seat. Rosa said no! She was arrested.

Rosa Parks started something! African Americans refused to ride the city buses for a year in the Montgomery Bus Boycott. Finally, the U.S. Supreme Court ruled that buses must be integrated.

Four college students sat down at a whites-only lunch counter in Greensboro, North Carolina. They refused to leave. Students at other colleges decided to hold "sit-ins" all over America!

Ruby Bridges was the first Black child to enter a white school in New Orleans, Louisiana. People yelled at her on the way to school, but she bravely attended her classes every day!

Both Black and white Americans rode buses in Freedom Rides from Washington, D.C. to the South. They went to the South to fight against discrimination.

Martin Luther King, Jr. made a famous speech at the March on Washington in 1963. He was the leader of the Civil Rights Movement. He asked people to be peaceful, not violent, in their protests.

Coretta Scott King was the wife of Martin Luther King, Jr. She founded the Martin Luther King, Jr. Center for Nonviolent Social Change. She worked for civil rights alongside her husband and after his death.

Reading tests and poll taxes kept many African Americans from voting in the South. During "Freedom Summer," volunteers worked hard to register Black citizens to vote!

In 1964 and 1965, Congress passed important laws to give African Americans equal rights. Freedoms and basic rights were now guaranteed by law!

Because of the hard work and sacrifices of those who fought for equal rights, African Americans have achieved great things in the United States of America!

Word Search!

The Civil Rights Movement truly changed America during the 20th century. Using the word bank, find the words that relate to some of the changes brought about by the Civil Rights Movement.

X	Z	X	E	X	Z	Y	A	M	V	Z	D	F
F	L	C	J	Y	L	Q	E	R	O	L	A	W
O	P	P	O	R	T	U	N	I	T	I	E	S
C	X	Z	I	E	I	I	O	N	I	J	F	L
F	Q	F	J	W	N	G	L	G	N	G	G	O
F	R	E	E	D	O	M	H	A	G	I	E	O
S	M	Z	G	T	C	J	W	T	U	W	B	H
R	M	P	L	C	P	E	A	E	S	Q	R	C
N	O	I	T	A	R	G	E	T	N	I	E	S
S	W	A	L	E	N	C	E	G	Z	B	I	U

Word Bank

LAWS	EQUALITY
RIGHTS	FREEDOM
VOTING	INTEGRATION
SCHOOLS	OPPORTUNITIES

Amazing Maze!

During the Montgomery Bus Boycott, African Americans ended up walking to work or wherever else they had to go. Help Rosa Parks find her way to work through the maze of streets.

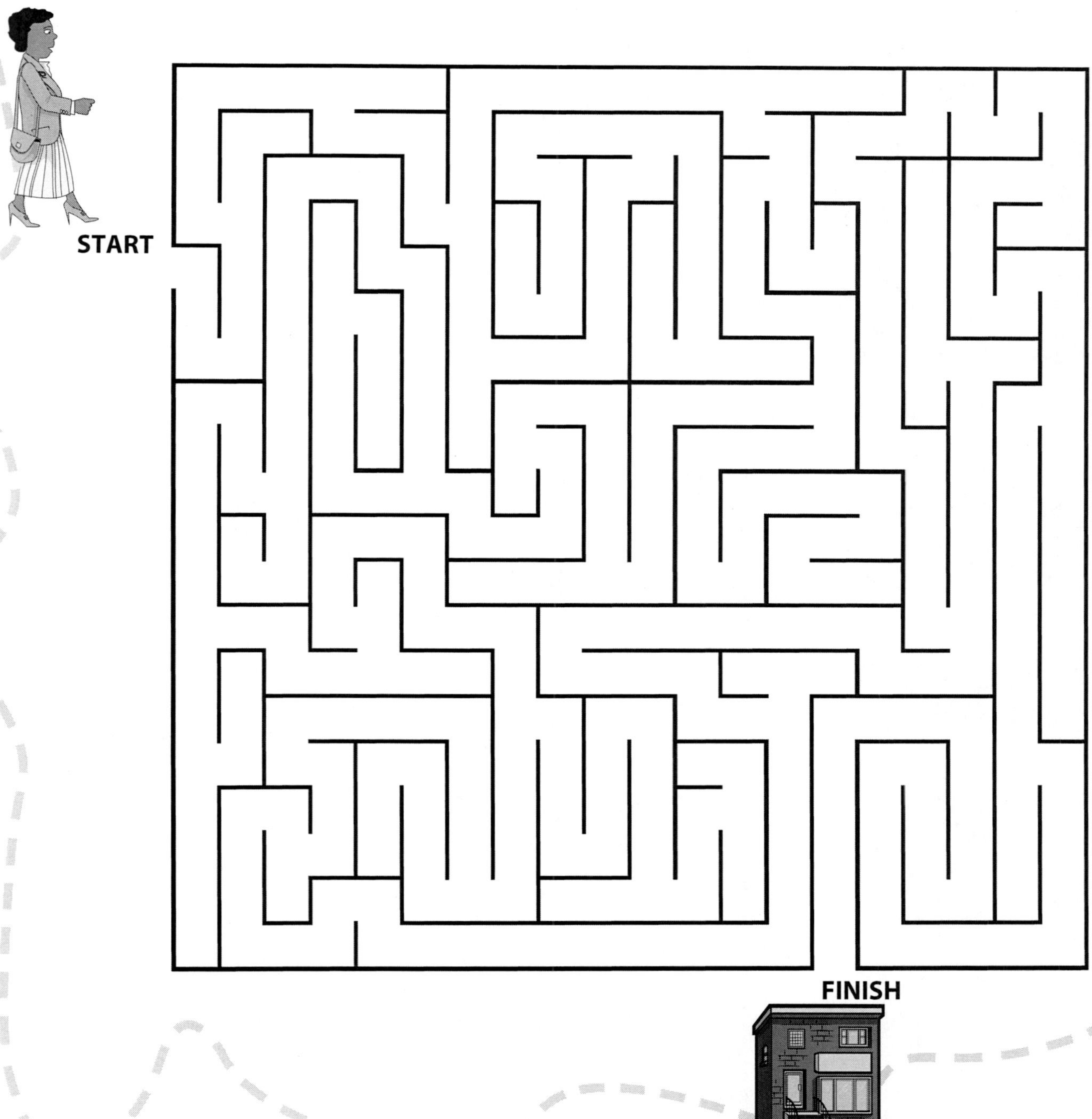

All Mixed-Up!

The First Amendment to the U.S. Constitution lists five basic rights that Americans have. Match each right below to the correct picture.

Freedom of speech

Freedom of the press

Freedom of religion

Freedom to assemble

Freedom to petition the government

Double Trouble!

The Civil Rights Movement brought an end to laws that separated Black and white Americans in public places. Before laws were changed, Black Americans even had to drink from separate water fountains. Find the picture that is different and circle it. Then, color them all.

Only Half the Picture!

Thurgood Marshall was a famous civil rights lawyer before he became the first African American U.S. Supreme Court Justice. The Supreme Court meets in a beautiful building in Washington, D.C. Draw the other half of the building and then color the whole thing.

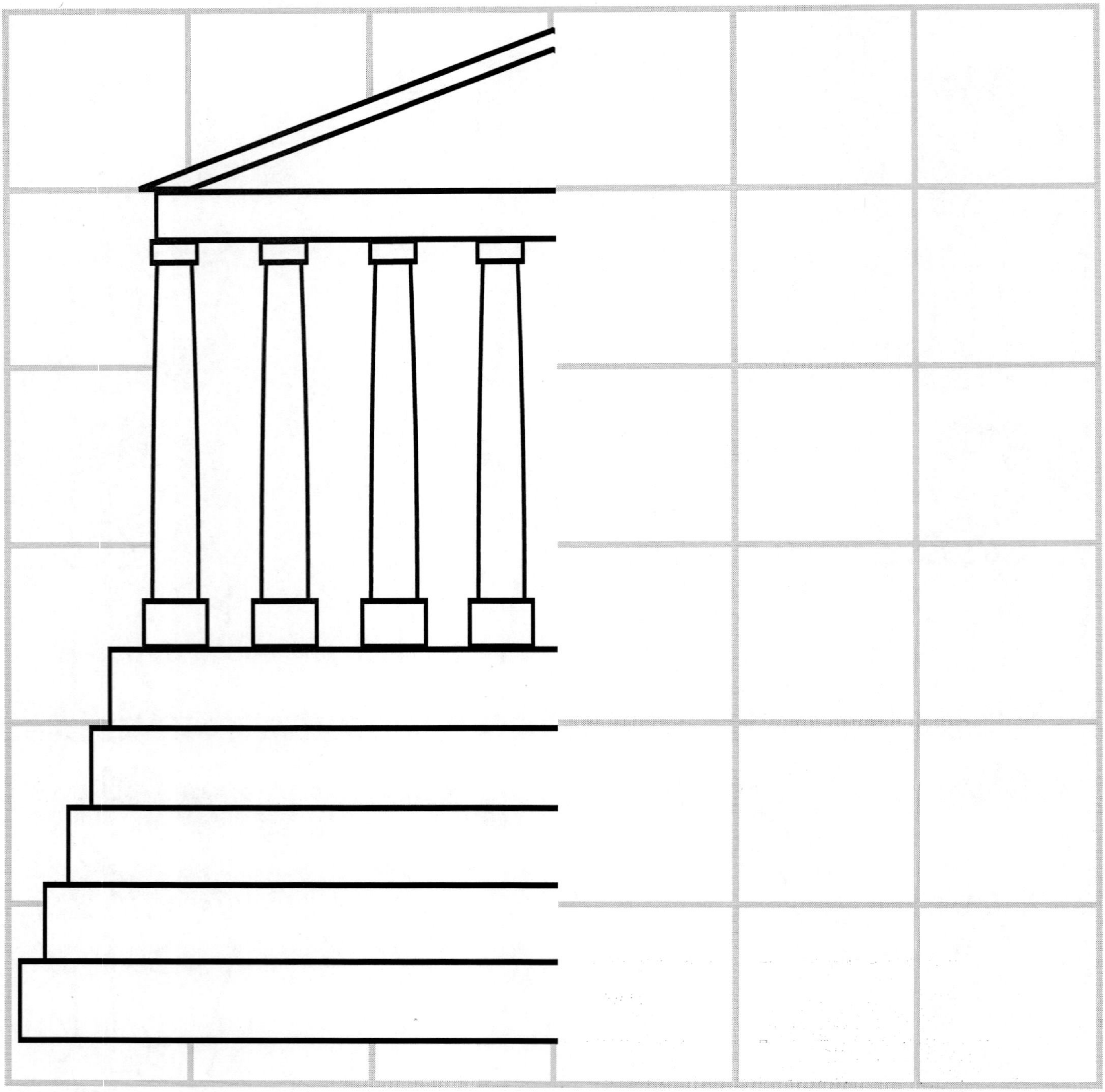

Connect the Dots!

Many of the Tuskegee Airmen became pilots, navigators, or bombardiers. Connect the dots to see what was on their emblem.

It's a Secret!

In 1964, this U.S. president signed the Civil Rights Act into law. Use the secret code to solve the puzzle and find out his name.

Secret Code

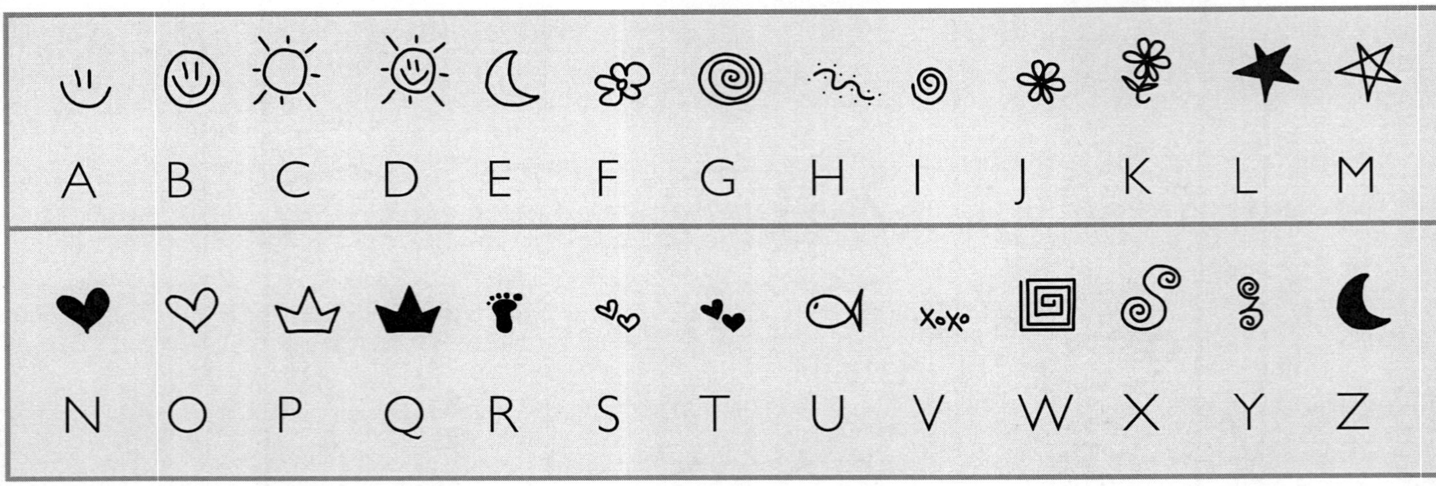

_____ _____ _____ _____ _____ _____

_____ _____ _____ _____ _____ _____ _____